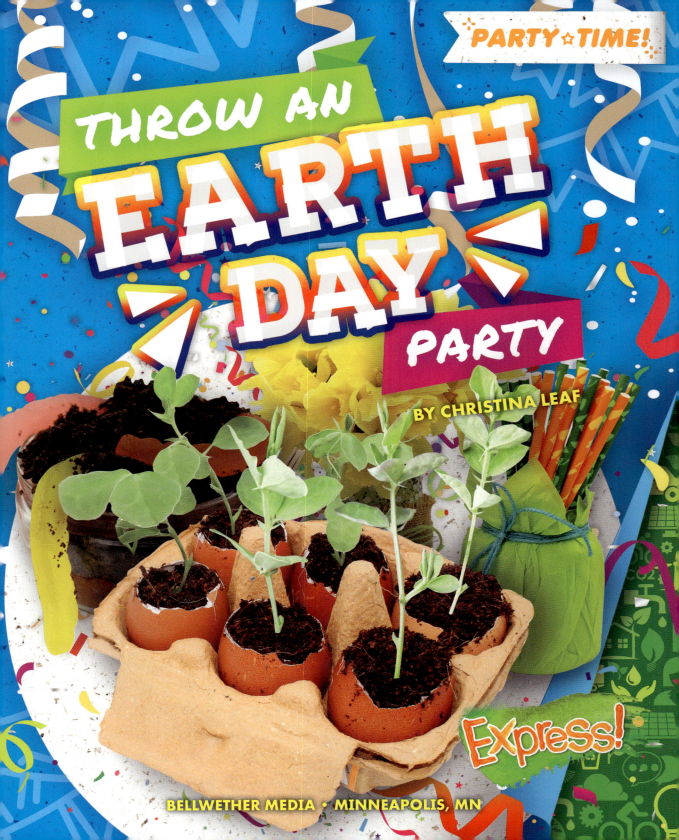

PARTY TIME!

THROW AN EARTH DAY PARTY

BY CHRISTINA LEAF

Express!

BELLWETHER MEDIA • MINNEAPOLIS, MN

Imagination comes alive in Express! Transform the everyday into the fresh and new, discover ways to stir up flavor and excitement, and experiment with new ideas and materials. Express! makerspace books: where your next creative adventure begins!

This edition first published in 2023 by Bellwether Media, Inc.

No part of this publication may be reproduced in whole or in part without written permission of the publisher. For information regarding permission, write to Bellwether Media, Inc., Attention: Permissions Department, 6012 Blue Circle Drive, Minnetonka, MN 55343.

Library of Congress Cataloging-in-Publication Data

LC record for Throw an Earth Day Party available at: https://lccn.loc.gov/2022047992

Text copyright © 2023 by Bellwether Media, Inc. EXPRESS and associated logos are trademarks and/or registered trademarks of Bellwether Media, Inc.

Editor: Elizabeth Neuenfeldt   Series Design: Jeffrey Kollock   Book Designer: Laura Sowers
Projects and Project Photography: Jessica Moon   Craft Instructions: Sarah Eason

Printed in the United States of America, North Mankato, MN.

TABLE OF CONTENTS

Throw an Earth Day Party!....4
Earth Day Bunting............6
Glass Jar Party Pots........10
Plant-based Sandwich Bar...12
Dirt Dessert!................16
Supergreen Smoothie......18
Eggshell Planters..........20
Glossary...................22
To Learn More............23
Index.....................24

THROW AN EARTH DAY PARTY!

Earth Day was first held on April 22, 1970. **Environmentalists** wanted a day to highlight the importance of **conservation**. Today, people celebrate by cleaning up parks, planting trees, and learning about Earth.

You can celebrate Earth Day by throwing an **eco-friendly** party! The activities in this book have been designed with our planet in mind. You will create decorations from recycled materials and make plant-based foods like sandwiches and smoothies. Get ready to throw an Earth Day party!

TOP TIP

Look for this feature throughout the book. It will give you tips to help improve your projects!

MATERIALS AND TOOLS

To make your party projects, you will need some basic art supplies, such as colored cardstock and paper. You will also need some basic kitchen tools, including knives, forks, spoons, cutting boards, and mixing and serving bowls.

You will also need:
- glue
- scissors
- pencils
- yarn
- paint
- paintbrushes
- hole punch

EARTH DAY BUNTING

Extra materials needed:
old cardboard, such as a cereal box
green and blue tissue paper
yarn
hole punch

Cardboard is one of the most recycled materials! Not all items that go in the recycling bin can be recycled. But in 2021, nearly all cardboard in the United States was recycled! Additionally, around half of all cardboard was made from recycled paper. You can decorate for your party with this bunting made from recycled cardboard!

1 Draw a triangle onto a piece of paper, then cut it out to make a triangle template.

2 Use your template to draw triangles onto your cardboard.

3 Cut out your triangles. You will need at least 10 to make a long enough bunting.

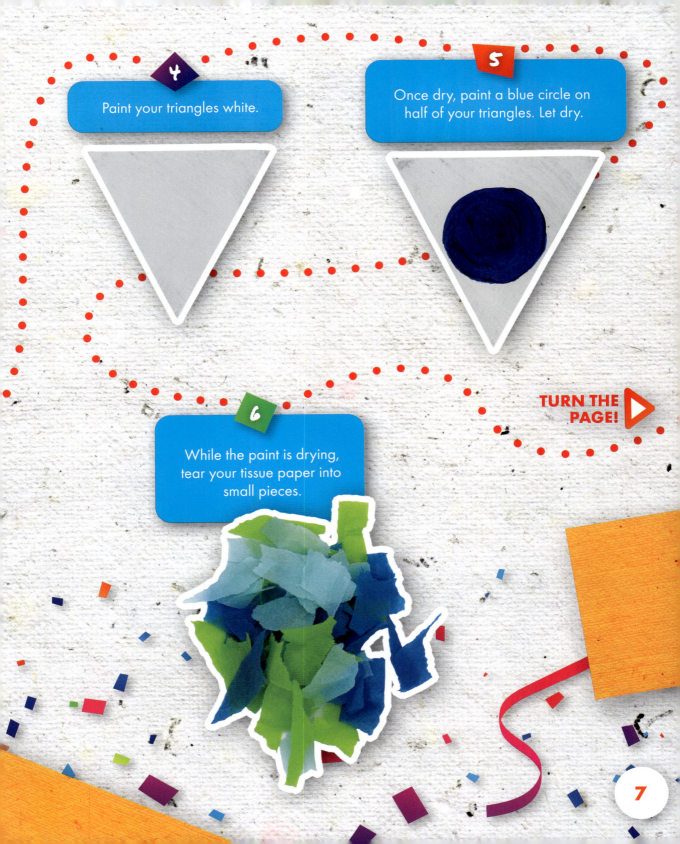

4 Paint your triangles white.

5 Once dry, paint a blue circle on half of your triangles. Let dry.

6 While the paint is drying, tear your tissue paper into small pieces.

TURN THE PAGE!

7
Glue the tissue pieces onto the triangles that do not have blue circles and let dry.

8
Use green paint to paint Earth's continents on the blue circles.

9
Once dry, use a hole punch to make a hole in each upper corner of the triangles.

TOP TIP

When you complete Step 10, make sure you tie a knot in both ends of the yarn to keep the triangles from falling off!

10

Thread the triangles onto a long piece of yarn, alternating between the two designs.

FINAL

GLASS JAR PARTY POTS

Extra materials needed:
3 glass jars
2 squares of tissue paper
colored yarn
recycled fabric,
 patterned and plain

Glass can be recycled over and over again! It can easily be crushed and remade into new glass. Some glass-making companies do this to use less energy and be eco-friendly. In this activity, you can make party decorations from glass jars. When the party is over, you can reuse the jars for something new!

1) Collect two short jars and one tall jar. Wash well.

2) Take one short jar and place it in the middle of a piece of tissue paper. Wrap all four corners up and around your jar.

3) Wrap a piece of yarn around the top of the jar and tie as shown to secure the tissue paper.

4 Repeat Steps 2 and 3 with the other short jar. Put both jars to one side.

5 Cut some patterned fabric into four squares. Tape the pieces to your tall jar.

6 Cut a length of plain fabric long enough to wrap around the jar. Tie yarn around the fabric to secure it. Fill your party pots with flowers, wooden cutlery, and paper drinking straws.

TOP TIP
When your party is over, remove the decorations from your jars and reuse them.

FINAL

PLANT-BASED SANDWICH BAR

Extra materials needed:
2 serving boards
3 reusable dishes
2 tomatoes
1 cucumber
5 falafels
hummus
10 beet slices
1 head of lettuce
1 red onion
6 plant-based cheese slices
1 avocado
6 bread slices
6 bagels
6 tortilla wraps

Eating **vegetarian** meals is good for the environment! Plant-based foods send fewer harmful gases into the **atmosphere** than animal-based foods. They use less land and water to grow, too. Most vegetarian meals also offer **nutrients** to keep bodies healthy and strong! Try making a delicious vegetarian sandwich from this plant-based sandwich bar!

SAFETY TIP
Ask an adult to help you with all of the steps that require a knife.

1 Slice your tomatoes, then place them on a serving board.

2 Slice your cucumber and place the slices below the tomatoes.

3 Put the falafels in a reusable dish, then place it on your board.

4 Fill another reusable dish with hummus. Place it on your board below the falafel.

5 Put the sliced beets in the final dish and place it below the hummus.

6 Tear your lettuce into pieces and wash well. Then, place them at the top right corner of your board.

TURN THE PAGE!

7
Cut the onion into slices and place them below your lettuce.

8
Place your plant-based cheese slices below the onion slices.

9
Cut the avocado in half and take out the pit. Cut the avocado into slices and place them on the bottom right corner of your board.

10
Arrange your bread, bagels, and wraps in rows on the second wooden board. Your sandwich bar is now ready to enjoy!

FINAL

DIRT DESSERT!

Extra materials needed:
18–20 chocolate cookies
1 packet instant chocolate pudding
milk (check pudding instructions)
1 packet of gummy worms
6 shallow reusable dishes
rolling pin
mixing bowl

Earthworms may be small, but they have a big effect on soil! They break down dead plants to give the soil more nutrients. Their **burrows** allow more air and water to get into the soil and help roots grow. You can make a delicious treat to honor these helpful animals with this fun activity!

1 Follow the instructions to prepare the chocolate pudding, then leave to set.

2 In a mixing bowl, crush the cookies with the end of a rolling pin.

3 Add a layer of pudding to each dish. Add a layer of crushed cookies on top. Add a second layer of pudding, filling the dish to the top.

layers

4 Place a few gummy worms on top of each dessert. Finally, sprinkle with some more crushed cookies. Yum!

TOP TIP

Serve immediately or keep in the fridge.

FINAL

17

SUPERGREEN SMOOTHIE

Extra materials needed:
1 avocado
5 strawberries
handful baby spinach
1/2 cup (150 ml) plain yogurt
2 oranges, juiced and grated
blender
6 drinking glasses
6 paper straws

Smoothies are a delicious way to drink your fruits and vegetables! Blended fruit drinks have been around for hundreds of years in many **cultures**. They became popular in the United States in the 1930s. People were able to buy electric blenders for their homes. This smoothie recipe tastes great and has the healthy benefits of spinach, oranges, and strawberries!

Ask an adult to help you cut the avocado in half. Remove the pit, scoop out the inside, and place in the blender cup.

2 Have an adult help you cut the tops off of the strawberries, then add to the blender cup.

3 Add the yogurt and a handful of baby spinach to the blender cup.

4
Add the orange juice and 1/2 teaspoon of grated zest.

5
Ask an adult to help you blend all the ingredients, then pour into two glasses and add drinking straws.

TOP TIP
Repeat the recipe two more times to make enough smoothies for six party guests.

FINAL

EGGSHELL PLANTERS

Extra materials needed:
packet of sweet pea seeds
peat-free compost
water
an old cardboard egg carton
6 eggshells

Many gardeners use compost in their gardens. **Compost** is made from **decayed** plants and other materials. It adds nutrients to the soil and helps keep plants healthy. Many cities in the United States have composting programs to keep food waste like apple cores and eggshells out of **landfills**. You and your guests can use compost materials to grow plants with this fun activity!

1
Carefully wash out your used eggshells.

2
Use a teaspoon to carefully fill the eggshells with compost.

GLOSSARY

atmosphere—the air surrounding Earth

burrows—holes or tunnels some animals dig in the earth

compost—plants and other materials that have broken down and can be used to help new plants grow

conservation—the preservation and protection of something, especially related to the environment and natural world

cultures—beliefs, arts, and ways of life in places or societies

decayed—broken down due to natural processes

eco-friendly—not harmful to the environment

environmentalists—people who study the environment and work to keep it clean

landfills—places where trash is buried in the ground

nutrients—substances that give energy and keep living things healthy

vegetarian—related to foods or meals that do not have meat in them

TO LEARN MORE

AT THE LIBRARY

Douglas, Paul. *A Kid's Guide to Saving the Planet: It's Not Hopeless and We're Not Helpless.* Minneapolis, Minn.: Beaming Books, 2022.

French, Jess. *What a Waste.* New York, N.Y.: DK Publishing, 2019.

Lindstrom, Carole. *We Are Water Protectors.* New York, N.Y.: Roaring Brook Press, 2020.

ON THE WEB

FACTSURFER

Factsurfer.com gives you a safe, fun way to find more information.

1. Go to www.factsurfer.com.

2. Enter "Earth Day party" into the search box and click 🔍.

3. Select your book cover to see a list of related content.

INDEX

April, 4
atmosphere, 12
cardboard, 6
compost, 20
conservation, 4
dirt dessert, 16–17
Earth Day bunting, 6–9
earthworms, 16
eggshell planters, 20–21
environmentalists, 4
glass, 10
glass jar party pots, 10–11
landfills, 20
materials and tools, 5
nutrients, 12, 16, 20
plant-based sandwich bar, 12–15
recycling, 4, 6, 10
safety tip, 12
smoothies, 18
supergreen smoothie, 18–19
top tip, 5, 8, 11, 17, 19
United States, 6, 18, 20
vegetarian, 12

All photos in this book are provided through the courtesy of Calcium.